Joseph and Me

IN THE DAYS OF THE HOLOCAUST

Joseph and Me
IN THE DAYS OF THE HOLOCAUST

by Judy Hoffman

Illustrations by Lili Cassel-Wronker

KTAV Publishing Company, Inc.

Design and Art Supervision by Ezekiel Schloss

Library of Congress Cataloging in Publication Data

Hoffman, Judy.
  Joseph and me.

  SUMMARY: The author describes her experiences
as a Jewish child living in hiding with a Dutch
family in Amsterdam during World War II.
Additional text and illustrations include further
details of the Nazi persecution of the Jews and
the fate of those that survived.
  1. Holocaust, Jewish (1939-1945)—Netherlands—
Amsterdam—Personal narratives—Juvenile literature.
2. Hoffman, Judy—Juvenile literature. 3. Jews
in Amsterdam—Biography—Juvenile literature.
4. Amsterdam—Biography—Juvenile literature.
[1. Holocaust, Jewish (1939-1945)—Netherlands—
Amsterdam—Personal narratives. 2. Jews in the
Netherlands. 3. Netherlands—History—German
occupation, 1940-1945] I. Cassel-Wronker, Lili,
1924-   II. Title.
D810.J4H62   940.53′1503′924   79-23800
ISBN 0-87068-655-0

Manufactured in the United States of America

CONTENTS

PROLOGUE

The Nazis and the Jews

Three generations of a European Jewish family; grandparents, parents and children.

Not too many years ago there were millions of Jews in the old countries of Europe. No matter which European country they lived in, and whether they were young or old, rich or poor, modern or *Hasidic,* city dwellers or villagers, they all belonged to one people—the Jewish people. Unlike the world's other peoples, all of whom had their own countries, the Jews had been living in foreign lands for more than two thousand years.

Jews first came to Europe in the time of the ancient *Romans.* By modern times there were more than eleven million Jews in the countries of Europe, far more than lived in any other part of the world.

Jewish victims of a pogrom.

The European Jews had the same traditions that present-day American and Israeli Jews have. They celebrated *Shabbat* (the Jewish Sabbath) as well as the Jewish High Holidays and the festivals of *Sukkot, Passover,* and *Shavuot.* They fasted on *Yom Kippur* and *Tisha B'av.* Their children attended Jewish schools. Perhaps they dressed differently, but the Jews of Europe lived, danced, and sang with a tremendous spirit that was filled with pride.

But it was not easy for the European Jews. Because of *anti-Semitism*—bigoted hatred of the Jews—they were a *persecuted* people. Around the supper table at night, the family would speak of the many kinds of discrimination against them because they were Jewish—*pogroms* and other unpleasant events.

Jewish teenagers in a Russian ghetto.

Why did many of their non-Jewish neighbors persecute the Jews? Because they were "different." But what was different about them? Weren't they human beings like all other people? Of course. The problem was—they followed a different religion and had many customs and practices that set them apart. People disliked the Jews because of these differences. They felt that the differences meant the Jews weren't as good as everyone else. There was very little the Jews could do about this. There was no Constitution, like ours in the United States, to protect the rights of all people. So the Jews had to be strong and courageous, for at any moment their non-Jewish neighbors might try to harm them.

Adolf Hitler and his generals.

In 1933, in Germany, an evil man named *Adolf Hitler* came to power. He and his supporters, who were called *Nazis*, hated the Jews. They wanted to destroy all the Jews of Europe. Unfortunately, many people laughed at Hitler. They knew he was anti-Semitic and they considered him crazy, but they felt he was no more harmful than a clown in a circus.

A Jewish family being sent to a concentration camp.

Soon everyone learned that Hitler was not joking. The Nazis fired all the German Jews from their jobs. Jewish children were thrown out of school. Jews were forced to sell their businesses. Some German Jews fled the country; others sent their children to neighboring countries like Holland and France. However, the Jews were not safe even in other parts of Europe.

Jews in the ghetto being threatened by the Nazis.

When World War II began in 1939, the Nazis conquered almost all of Europe. Jews in the countries of Poland, Czechoslovakia, Hungary, Russia, Holland, Belgium, Italy, France, and Greece fell into the hands of the evil Nazis. First, the Nazis made all Jews wear yellow stars on their clothing. Then they forced the Jews into certain neighborhoods in towns and cities. These Jewish areas were called *ghettos*.

Jewish prisoners being marched to the death camp.

Life in the ghettos was very difficult. There wasn't enough food for everyone. The Nazis turned off the water and the electricity in some ghettos. But despite the constant fear, hunger, and disease, the Jews managed to survive. Children went to special schools so that Jewish learning would continue. Their parents tried to find enough food to avoid starvation.

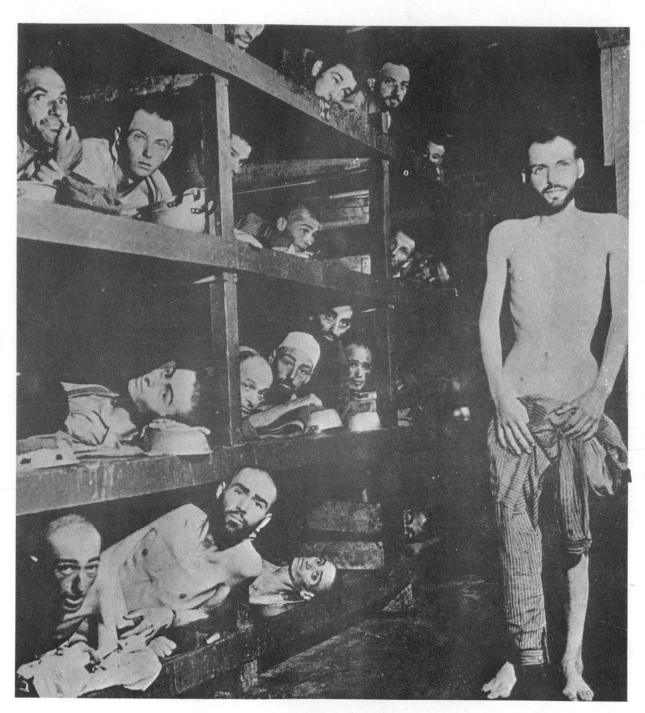

Prisoners in a typical concentration camp.

Nevertheless, many Jews died in the ghetto. When they were sick, there was no medicine to take. Sometimes there was nothing to eat for days and days. Men, women, and children died of starvation and disease. Some were so weak that they collapsed and died right on the streets.

Jewish children. Victims of the "final solution" begging for a crust of bread.

Starvation, disease, and other *"natural"* causes did not work fast enough for the Nazis. They wanted to get rid of all the Jews as quickly as possible, so they decided to take direct action to kill them. The Nazis called this decision the *"final solution,"* because once it was completed there would no longer be a Jewish "problem" in Europe—there would no longer be a Jewish "problem" because there would be no Jews. It didn't matter how old or how young the victims were—no one was spared. Everyone who was Jewish had to die.

15

Before entering the gas chamber, this Jew recites his final prayers.

At first the Nazis began marching the Jews to big ditches outside the towns and villages. Then they shot them and buried the bodies. But even this method wasn't fast enough for the Nazis. So they set up *concentration camps*. Jews were taken to the camps on special trains. Once there the Nazis told them to undress so they could take showers after their long journey. But the shower room was actually a gas chamber. When the people went in they were killed by poison gas. Afterwards their bodies were burned and their ashes were scattered on the ground.

Nazis attacking the Warsaw ghetto. Notice the Jewish soldier who commits suicide by jumping from a building rather than fall into the hands of the Nazis.

Not all the Jews of Europe died in the concentration camps. In Warsaw and other ghettos brave Jews fought back. Almost unarmed and outnumbered more than 10 to 1, the ghetto fighters inspired the whole world by their courage. The tale of their heroism made all Jews proud. The Nazis thought the Jews wouldn't defend themselves, but the ghetto heroes proved that Jews would fight for their lives, their families, and their God. Other Jewish fighters, called *partisans*, kept up the battle even after the ghettos were destroyed. They hid in the countryside and attacked the Germans whenever they could. The ghetto resistance fighters and the partisan guerillas made at least some Nazis pay for the "final solution."

When the war ended in 1945, nearly six million Jewish men, women, and children had been killed by the Nazis. We call this event the *Holocaust*. Never in history has one people suffered such a loss. We must always remember their agony and suffering. We must never forget the six million Jews who died during the Holocaust. There are many tales of the Holocaust, and *Joseph and Me* is one such story. Read it and remember the mothers and fathers, sisters and brothers, aunts and uncles, grandfathers and grandmothers who died during the Holocaust.

JOSEPH AND ME

It Is Time to Share My Story

I was a small child then, and I am grown up now. I live here in the United States and am married to a good and loving man. I have two beautiful children whom I love very much, and my life revolves around them and their activities. I take care of my family and my home much as other mothers do, but I am different. I am different because deep down inside me I have a story which pushes at my heart. Sometimes it pushes so hard, it brings tears to my eyes, and then it stops pushing for a little while. It has been pushing very hard lately, and I have decided that it is time to share my story. Perhaps the pushing will stop then. I do have one wish before I share. I choose to share my book only with children. They will say they have never heard such a story, yet I know they must not live out their lives without hearing it. I believe it will push at their hearts too, and then bring tears to their eyes, for my story has pain in it. But learning anything new has pain in it, and without learning, how can we understand the way in which to go?

The German Invasion

It was May, and the year was 1940. My foster sister, Gerda, and I ran to the window. What an unbelievable sight! Everywhere I looked, just as far as I could see, the sky was covered with men floating slowly down to earth. They were hanging from strings with puffy round pillows attached to the strings. Gerda said they were parachutes, but they looked like spacemen to me. I loved watching them float.

Gerda and I ran down the stairs from our apartment and into the street. We danced from the door entrance across the street to the canal and then back again. We danced while we watched the pillow men land and roll up their pillow parachutes. We probably would have danced forever, but the planes came.

Annie screamed at us from the second-story window, "Hurry, come into the house immediately!"

We obeyed her, but oh, how slowly we walked, for we didn't want to miss one single thing that was happening in our usually quiet city of Amsterdam. As the planes drew closer and their sounds became loud, we moved quicker and quicker. Now we ran to get back to Annie and took the hallway stairs two at a time. She met us halfway down before we could even reach the apartment. She grabbed our arms and almost dragged us back down the stairs into the hall on the first floor. I wanted one more peek at the planes, but her large strong hand around my arm wouldn't let me escape.

As yet, there were no bomb shelters in Amsterdam, and the people used hallways on the ground floors of their buildings to help protect them from falling bombs. Annie said that bombs were dropping nearby, and I could hear the loud explosions as they smashed into the ground. Perhaps I should have been afraid, but I wasn't. There were five other families sitting together in the hallway with us, and since Gerda and I were the youngest, everyone tried to entertain us during the air raid. They played many guessing games with us and gave us large chunks of chocolate. Warm thick cocoa from a blue-covered pitcher was poured into small mugs for us, and when we became irritable, they found more goodies in their pockets to bribe us and distract us from the bombing.

The first air raid was exciting, but after that, even the chocolate did not please me any longer, and I would become tired quickly. Sometimes I would lean against Annie and try to go to sleep. I liked to rest next to her fat body, for she was warm and soft. There were air raids every day now, and I hadn't thought about Joseph at all. . . .

He was living in Amsterdam, too. He had a foster family like mine, and they lived just a few miles away from me. I needed to see him just to talk about Papa and Mama, but I wasn't able to. As I leaned against Annie, I began to think back to the last time we had been together with Papa. It was at the train station. Papa had kissed us and told us how much he loved us. He had reminded us again that no matter what happened, we were never to forget the night of terror called Kristallnacht. He told us he would come for us as soon as he and Mama were able to. I did not know then that those were the last words Papa would ever say to us.

Kristallnacht

My real mother was named Else, and my father was Jacob. Joseph and I were their only children. Although it is now many years later, I still remember our last days together. It all began on a Tuesday—the ninth of November, 1938. We were living in Germany then. We had heard that the German soldiers disliked the Jews, but many of us, including my parents, were not certain whether this was really true. If the Jewish people were uncertain, what happened that night changed their minds. Ever since, that night has been called Kristallnacht, which in German means "The Night of Broken Glass," because throughout Germany Jewish windows were broken. Papa told us never to forget Kristallnacht, but I wouldn't be able to forget it even if I wanted to.

It seems that a seventeen-year-old Jewish boy named Herschel Grynszpan, who was living in Paris, received a letter from his father. The sad letter described how the Germans had made his family suffer. Herschel became very upset. He bought a pistol and went to the German embassy in Paris. He had wanted to see the ambassador but, instead, met with Ernst vom Rath, a minor official. He shot him, and two days later, on November ninth, Vom Rath died. Although the Germans had already planned Kristallnacht, they used this incident as an excuse for beginning the terrible events.

German soldiers broke into Jewish houses all over Germany. They set fires, they murdered, they arrested, and they stole. They broke windows in stores owned by Jews, and in our homes too. They threw belongings that people loved and treasured out into the streets. Then they poured gasoline on them and set them afire. They ripped pictures and broke antique chairs. They broke valuable china dishes and crystal lamps, and they destroyed books. They threw out hundreds of books with favorite fairy tales and folktales, history books, music books, art albums, and Bibles. It took no time before the flames in the streets grew enormous. The broken glass from all the store windows reflected the fires and made them appear even larger and brighter.

Papa was a caretaker in the small synagogue of our town, Goch. We lived in three small rooms near the top of the synagogue, and Papa's job was to care for the needs of the worshippers and keep the synagogue clean. I liked living there, for when I was in bed and almost asleep, I liked to hear the men downstairs praying during the late Sabbath service. It made me feel close to God, and the darkness no longer frightened me.

We didn't expect the German soldiers to come into our sacred synagogue, and we were very alarmed when they broke down the heavy doors that night. I remember there were so many of them! I could see them from upstairs. They laughed loudly, and they shouted as they ripped the beautiful blue-and-gold velvet curtains from the Holy Ark where the Torah Scrolls were kept. Mama had sewed them for many months before she felt they were ready to cover the sacred Ark. The soldiers didn't stop there. They poured gasoline onto the Torahs and set fire to them. It was then that Papa began to cry and ran toward the burning Torahs. When the soldiers turned and saw him, they knocked him down with their rifles and dragged him outside. Papa was arrested that night and we didn't know what to do. Mama cried and told us not to be afraid. I didn't know how not to be afraid, for I was more frightened that night than I had ever been in my entire life. All I remember from then on is that I cried and cried. I tried to sleep. Mama rocked me, but I could not stop crying.

Papa came home eighteen hours later and told us that two of our friends had been killed by the Germans just a few hours before. Kristallnacht is a terrible memory, one I shall never forget.

I did not know that Papa and Mama were now very worried for our safety. Although we were very young—Joseph was ten and I was six—our parents decided that we would be safer outside Germany, even if it meant being separated from them, so plans were made to send us to Holland. Papa spoke to aunts and uncles who lived in or near Goch, and someone sent a message to someone else in Holland. Because Goch was quite close to the Dutch border, the plans were completed quickly. Before we knew what was happening, Mama packed small bags for each of us, telling us over and over again not to be afraid. She told us that she and Papa would come to get us as soon as possible, and then we would all go to England to live.

Papa took us to the station and helped us onto the train. He kissed us and squeezed us too hard. He told us he would see us very soon. As the train moved out, we waved and waved until we could no longer see him or the other parents standing waving next to him. Then we turned and looked around. The train was filled with children! No grown-ups, only children! I saw nine of my cousins sitting near Joseph and me. Joseph was always teasing me at home, but this time he just sat next to me and held my hand so I would not cry. I almost didn't, but the tears ran down my cheeks as I said the special prayer called the *Shema*.

I was asleep when the train came to a halt in Soesterdijk, a border town in Holland. Nine people met us, four men and five women. They were in charge of taking all seventy-six children from the train to our first orphanage. I learned that the orphanage was called a waiting station, because we were to be there only a short time before moving on to a more permanent orphanage in Amsterdam.

We were piled into old cars and trucks and rode over bumpy roads for about twenty minutes. Then we arrived at a large, barnlike building with a very steep roof. It was so steep that the sides seemed to be dripping onto the street. The front windows looked like yawns from mouths, and the large door matched the windows. Inside, the rooms were very big. The dining room and the kitchen were just one long room, and there were many oval tables set up with chairs around them. At the end of the room was a higher table. It was here that huge kettles of food would be placed for meals. We would learn to stand in line, pick up a tin plate, and hold it out for a scoop of food from the large kettles.

Upstairs, there were two dormitory rooms with cots in them. We were allowed to choose any place we wished to sleep. Underneath each cot was a large drawer attached to the floor. Joseph and I put all our things into one drawer and chose beds next to each other.

The day went by slowly. There was very little to do except play with each other and have our meals. We were not allowed to leave the building without permission. Even then, only seven of us could go into the garden at one time to get some fresh air. I missed Mama and Papa so much at night that I could not always fall asleep. I would see the Torahs burning again, and I would begin to cry. One night I heard Joseph crying, but that was the only time. He was very brave.

We were at Soesterdijk for seven long months. One day, in the midst of play, we were told to pack our belongings. We would soon be leaving for Amsterdam on the train. We were somehow glad to be leaving, although no one had been unkind to us. It was just that we couldn't do anything. We couldn't go to school. We couldn't see our parents. We couldn't play outside. We didn't know what was happening in Germany to the Jews. Worst of all, we were afraid most of the time, and we were unsure what frightened us. To be thinking of moving again was good for us.

When we boarded the train this time, I noticed there were many more children. They were not just from Goch now, but from all over Germany. As the train pulled out, there was no one to wave to, and I thought of Papa waving at the station.

As the train passed through Holland, we looked out the windows. How beautiful it was! We saw the dikes and the canals, and the children skating. We saw mothers and fathers skating, too. It seemed as if everyone in Holland skated. I smiled when I thought of my mother or father skating. Papa was a very fine synagogue caretaker, but I do not think he would have been able to skate. Mama milked cows and cleaned and cooked and helped to take care of the synagogue, but I was sure she had never tried to ice-skate. It did look like fun, and I was sure that when they came to Holland to get Joseph and me, they would try skating for a bit. I watched the endless canals as the train moved toward Amsterdam. The frozen ice glistened and reflected the sun onto the train windows. I thought of Kristallnacht, and I began to shiver.

My New Home

We arrived in Amsterdam late in the afternoon and boarded wagons that would take us to our second orphanage. When we got there two hours later, I was surprised to see how different this house was from our first one. The roof was not steep, but instead had barely any slant to it at all. It was made of bricks, and each square window had pretty, pull-back curtains. There were empty flower boxes attached to the windows, and circles of dirt beneath them where flowers would be planted in the spring. In front of the house was an old hitching post where our driver tied his horse.

Inside the house it was quite lovely. The dormitory rooms where we would sleep had wallpaper with colored tulips on it. There were blue-and-white tiles on the walls of the bathrooms and white tiles on the floors. Large green towels hung through wooden loops near the bathroom doors. It was a clean house, and Mama would have been pleased to know that Joseph and I were there.

Our first day was a busy one. We had to put our things away in little chests of drawers. Joseph and I were not allowed to sleep in the same room, for the boys slept in one place and the girls in another. I did not like this because I wanted to be near Joseph at night. He was slow in unpacking and I had to wait for him. When he finally finished, we went into the kitchen. A nice old woman, wearing a long dress, a Dutch cap, and wooden shoes, told us to sit down at one of the tables. She brought us big mugs of hot coffee with heavy cream floating on top. She scooped two spoonfuls of sugar into each mug before pushing them toward us. Then she placed a muffin next to the mugs, and left. The coffee warmed me, and the muffin tasted very good. It took only a few minutes before the mugs were empty and the muffins gone. It made us both sleepy and we were ready for bed. The old lady returned, and told us to wash up in the bathroom, fold our clothes, and climb into bed. I was irritable because I couldn't sleep next to Joseph, and when the lights were turned off, I kept thinking of Mama and Papa. In the morning, when I awakened, my bed was wet.

Mama had given me a sewing needle and four spools of thread to mend our clothes if they became torn. I had three small tears in my dress and one in my slip, so I mended them my first day. Joseph had tears in his clothes too, but he wouldn't let me mend them. He said he was too busy to give them to me. I followed him around most of that first day, for there was nothing much to do. Joseph had already made some new friends, and it was hard to keep up with them as they played. Finally, I went back to my cot to resew my tears. I would have stayed with Joseph longer if I had known that I would be leaving the orphanage that very day.

It was July 1939 when I met my foster father. His name was Is. He and his wife had just one daughter of their own, and they had come to the orphanage a few weeks earlier to request a girl as a playmate for her. Is knew that all the children in the orphanage were Jewish, but this pleased him. He had known many Jews in Amsterdam, Jews who were people just like everyone else. They worked hard at their jobs and loved their families just as he did. The war had made life very difficult for them, and now he would be able to help them in his own way.

I had been selected as Gerda's new playmate and would be going to a new home before I had really gotten settled into this one. There were fifty-four of us in this second orphanage; others had been placed in another home several miles away. Everyone said that most of us would not get foster homes, for it was very difficult to find families to take Jewish children. I was considered lucky. I did not feel lucky that day as I prepared to leave Joseph and the orphanage, however.

It would be many years before I learned that Joseph and I were the only children of the fifty-four to live through the Holocaust.

My foster father called me Dotje. I knew that I was going to like him, and I was certain that my real father would have liked him too. I hugged Joseph many times before my new parent beckoned me to come. We walked toward an old yellow bicycle, and Papa Is lifted me into the deep basket attached to the front of the bike. He hooked my suitcase over the edge of the handlebars and climbed on. As Papa Is pedaled rapidly down the cobblestone streets, I could feel my teeth rattle. I watched the crooked houses fly past us on one side and the market boats float down the canal on the other. The time went fast, and I was unprepared for the sudden stop. I almost became dislodged from my basket as we pulled up to my new home.

Papa Is helped me out of the basket and placed me on the sidewalk. He pointed to the window of a two-story apartment house. "That's where we live," he said. The building was quite tall and was attached to other tall apartment houses. Each apartment roof was separate from the one next to it and was very steep. Ours had a small Dutch flag at the top. It had three stripes across it, one red, one white, and one blue. The wind was blowing it in little gusts, and it seemed to bounce when hit by a puff of wind.

We pulled the bicycle into the hallway of our building and climbed the stairs. As we reached the top of the landing, Annie opened the door. I hadn't expected her to be so tall. She was taller than Papa Is. In fact, she was taller than any mother I had ever seen. "Welcome to our home, Dotje," she said as she bent down to kiss my hair. As I said, "Thank you," I noticed that she wore gold wire-rimmed glasses low on her nose. She was able to look either through them or over them. I wished it weren't impolite to giggle at her, for she made me want to laugh. Annie took my hand and walked into the small bedroom where Gerda was standing. She introduced me and told me that

Gerda and I would be playmates. I was to sleep in Gerda's room so that she would not be lonely anymore. Gerda was not pretty. Nothing seemed to match on her face. Her eyes weren't even, her nose wasn't slanted straight, and her lips never closed completely. She was tall like Annie, and her arms looked very long. She said hello to me and then turned back to her dolls. And what dolls they were! I had never seen such lovely ones. There were mama dolls and baby dolls and girl dolls and boy dolls. Each one was dressed in embroidered Dutch clothes which Papa Is had made, for he was a tailor. I had never had a doll in my life and I hoped Gerda would let me play with hers.

Annie called me into the kitchen and told me to sit down. She brought two mugs of coffee with sugar and heavy cream to the table, and Papa Is and I sat down to drink it. It smelled good, and I let the steam from the coffee float up my nose. We also had two sugar crisp wafers to dip in our coffee if we wished. As I sat at the table, I looked around. I could see that the apartment was not very big, and I thought it was quite nice of this family to take in another person with such a small apartment. I looked toward the kitchen. It had a sink against one wall with curtains draped around the lower part. There was a small white porcelain table next to the sink. It was where Annie prepared the meals. Near the table was a blue icebox with a drip pan underneath. One room served as both dining room and living room. The dining room table was large and round with legs which bent into circles at the bottom. There was a narrow couch with three green cushions on it and a shaggy gold afghan folded across the back. A small table stood next to the couch, and a brass lamp with a fringed lampshade had been placed in the center. I watched the fringes bounce in the breeze like the flag on the rooftop. It was a nice home, but a very tiny one. I would have to be very good so that my new foster family would keep me until my Mama and Papa came to Holland to get Joseph and me.

While I sipped my coffee, Annie spoke with me. She told me that she was very happy to have a playmate for Gerda; she was sure I would be happy too. She told me that I would have chores to do every day, but I knew about chores and was glad to have something to keep me busy. I would be expected to wash all the dishes after each meal and wet mop the kitchen floor each morning. I was to put Gerda's toys away after she had finished playing with them and put her dirty clothes into the hamper each night. I told Annie I would work very hard to be a good playmate for Gerda and would do my chores well too.

I was pleased when it was time to wash up for bed, for I was quite tired. When I climbed into my small bed next to Gerda's, I thought I had never been so far away from Joseph, and I missed him. Fortunately, I fell asleep before the tears in my head came into my eyes, but when I awoke in the morning, my bed was wet. I tried to hide it from Annie, but she discovered it anyway. She looked so tall when she told me that I mustn't do that any more. I was ashamed and told her that I couldn't help it, but I would try to never let it happen again.

After a breakfast of rolls, sweet butter, and rich coffee, I washed the dishes. Papa Is brought me a little stool to stand on so I could reach the sink more easily. Annie made the beds while Gerda got dressed. Papa Is was already dressed and getting ready to begin his work. He worked right in the house. He was a good tailor, and he made clothes for many people in the neighborhood. He said that he would begin to make some new clothes for me that very day.

After the dishes, I began to clean Gerda's room. I liked doing it because she had such lovely toys and I could handle them all when I put them away. Sometimes she would let me play with them for a bit, but more often than not, she chose to keep them from me. Annie never interfered when Gerda showed bad manners, but I knew my Mama would never have permitted someone not to share in our house. This wasn't our house, though, and Annie wasn't my Mama. I remembered to try to be grateful that I had a place to stay until Mama and Papa could take me to England.

When I finished my chores, Gerda and I went outside to play. Papa Is and Annie were planning to send us to school in just a few days, and then there would be no time for play. We crossed the street and walked to the edge of the canal, where we could see the small, flat market boats pass by. The day was warm, and the time passed quickly as we waved to the people on the boats and counted the bicycles on the street behind us. I liked spending time by the canal and was not anxious to go to school.

It began the following week. Gerda and I would be in first grade and would go to school each day. Papa Is said I would learn to read, and that pleased me. He finished my first dress. It was beautiful. He had remade one of Gerda's old dresses to fit me and added dotted lace around the waist like a belt.

I liked my new dress. It made me think of the High Holy Days with Mama and Papa in Goch. My Holy Day dress was dark-blue velvet with three white flowers near the neck. Mama made it for me, and I was allowed to wear it on Rosh Hashanah and Yom Kippur, the two most solemn holidays of the Jewish year. I didn't even have to change my beautiful dress when I helped Mama prepare the holiday meals. We ate chunks of delicious round challah, the special holiday bread, covered with golden honey. We ate ground apples with pieces of cloves in them. The honey and apples were meant to symbolize a sweet year, for Rosh Hashanah is the Jewish New Year festival. Then we ate spicy, stringy meat with tiny cold potatoes. Holiday services started early in our synagogue, and we could hear the people praying all day long as we moved about our rooms high above the sanctuary. I could remember so much. . . .

There were thirty children in our classroom, mostly boys. We studied numbers and letters and about the country of Holland. I worked very hard and could hardly believe it when it was time to go home. It was a good first day.

The days flew by now, and I continued to work and work. I didn't even notice that by Friday, only nineteen children were attending school. Our teacher noticed, however, and tried to teach us more and more in the short time we spent with her each day. The lessons were becoming more difficult, but I didn't mind for I wanted to learn to read as soon as possible. When the second Friday came, and Papa Is told us it was our last day, I cried. I didn't care that there were only seven children left, I wanted to attend. But that was not my choice.

Papa Is told me that I had been such a good girl in school, he was going to buy a book for me. He said it would be my very own and he would teach me to read as though I were in school. He did as he said and bought me a book two days later. I remember that its cover was blue, but I have forgotten its name. The part I do remember is that Annie would not let me read my new book. She said there was no time for such foolishness when there was so much to do. Papa Is said nothing, and I never read my first book.

Summer went by quickly, and then one day Papa Is told me it was time to visit Joseph. It was the month of September and there was a chill in the air as we bicycled to the town square. We met both Joseph and his foster father. While the two men talked, we hugged and hugged, and I cried. I was so happy to see him that I didn't know what to tell him first. Joseph was not speechless—he chattered away. He said his foster parents were Christian, just like mine. They tried to be good to him, he told me, but sometimes he misbehaved. He said more, lots more, but I don't remember it all. I only remember that Papa Is said it was time to go, and the time had gone all too quickly. My heart pounded as we parted, and then it just ached. When we arrived home, Annie gave us our usual mugs of hot coffee and heavy cream. It tasted good. While we were drinking, Annie said she had an idea. My birthday was coming next week, and she thought I should have a party.

A party! My very own party! I had never had one before, and I was unbelievably excited. Annie said she would make a birthday cake, and that I could invite the neighborhood children and those whom Gerda and I had met in school. I did as she said and eleven children said they would come to my party. Annie made a cake and it was beautiful. She placed it in the icebox until the next day, when she planned to pour some sugary icing and jam on it. Gerda told me that she would pick up her own toys on my birthday, and Papa Is said he would help me dry the dishes.

As I climbed into bed, I could not believe I would be seven years old when I awakened. I wished that Joseph could come to my party, but I had been afraid to ask for him. It was hard to fall asleep that night, and when I did, I had both good dreams and bad ones. When morning came, my bed was wet. I was frightened when I saw what I had done, for I knew it would make Annie angry. She came in to wish me happy birthday, and then saw my bed. She looked so tall to me as she told me how poorly I had behaved for someone who had just turned seven, and she ended by saying I could not have my party. In addition, I would have to call everyone myself and tell them why they couldn't come. What an awful day it was! I did not like being seven at all.

The next day Papa Is told me he had bought me a present before the party had been canceled, and now he didn't know what to do with it. He said it would please him if I would take his present. It was another lovely book. I loved Papa Is very much that day, and I planned to keep his book forever.

Just Waiting

Without school, the days passed slowly. I did my chores in the morning and then played with Gerda. Papa Is must have known we were too idle, and one day he came home with two pairs of ice skates. Gerda and I were very excited and ran to get our coats so we could go with Papa Is to the canal to try them. I had never been ice skating before and was breathless as he tied the skates onto my shoes. He helped Gerda, and then tied some large ones onto his own shoes. It took us several minutes before we could get our balance to stand up alone. Gerda was able to let go of Papa Is before I was. She even took a few awkward steps by herself, but when I tried, I fell down. He let me get up by myself, but I fell down again and again. By the end of the day, I could take a few steps without falling onto the hard ice.

We skated almost every day for the next few weeks. Gradually, I learned to move over the ice almost as well as Gerda and Papa Is. I thought it peculiar that so many grown-ups went to work each day on their ice skates. Mama and Papa would have laughed to see so many people skating up and down the canals. They would also have been pleased to hear me speak Dutch now. I guess it was because I was so young that I had almost forgotten my German. Even when I was with Joseph, we had spoken only Dutch.

As I thought about Mama and Papa, I realized today was Friday. In Goch, Papa would be getting the synagogue ready for the Sabbath service. Mama would be preparing cholent—a rich, thick bean stew with meat in it that would remain in the oven until Sabbath lunch time. She would take two freshly baked challahs out of the oven and would bring them to me to smell if I were there. I would have been mixing the baked apples and stewed pears together in a bowl for our dessert. Joseph would have been putting the laundry away, and then he would be sent to the tub for his bath. I could almost reach out and touch my thoughts . . .

Annie knew he was coming and Papa Is knew too, but I didn't. When I saw him, I froze for a minute, and then leaped at Joseph. I tried to smother him with kisses and hugs, but he didn't like all that mushy stuff and he pulled away. He certainly wasn't Sabbath-clean now! His neck needed scrubbing and his fingernails were dirty. His clothes didn't fit well either. Papa Is made my clothes, but Joseph's foster father was not a tailor. Joseph's shirt was too tight, his pants were too short. I sniffled a little as we talked, and Joseph wiped two tears from my face with his shirt tail. He told me things were just fine with him, and I said the same. We both knew differently, but we said nothing. I told him I could skate well now, and he said he could play chess. He asked me if I had been called a dirty Jew yet, and I told him I hadn't. We said more, but I don't remember what. Then there was a knock at the door, and Joseph's foster father took him away.

I wet my bed again that night, but I didn't care what Annie would say. There had been so much to think about before I fell asleep, and it had just happened. Joseph needed to remember to wash himself better. He needed Mama to remind him. And Papa would probably have to reteach him his blessings and prayers, but Papa would be patient with him. I remembered how carefully Joseph had copied Papa on those Sabbaths back home. Joseph had his own special wine cup, and he would recite the kiddush blessing over wine just like Papa. And I used to watch my Mama's face as she kindled the Sabbath lights. She looked so beautiful, so peaceful just then. What was the blessing she used to recite? I tried hard to remember . . . And the songs, the beautiful Sabbath songs we sang during and after the meal. How happy we were then.

When I finally fell asleep that night, I dreamed my thoughts. I was home with Mama and Papa and was in my own bed. I snuggled against my puffy quilt until I was toasty warm. I pulled the quilt over my head and then uncovered myself with tiny tugs of my toes. I could see the shadows of Mama's Sabbath candles reflecting on my wall. I heard Mama and Papa speaking to each other in low voices, but I could not hear what they were saying. Suddenly, my dream broke apart like a puzzle exploding, and I was being pushed on my ice skates down one of the long canals in Amsterdam. The canal just went on and on, without an end. I tried to turn myself around, but my skates would only go in one direction—away from Mama and Papa.

When I awoke, I was leaning against Annie. We were still in the hallway, waiting for the German planes to stop dropping their bombs on us.

My Star of David

I didn't like the Germans. They had frightened us during Kristallnacht and burned the Torahs in our synagogue. They had arrested Papa and many of our friends. I was afraid now as I listened to Annie and Papa Is talk about them. Gerda and I sat motionless, for we knew it was no time for foolishness and disobedience. We had not been sent to bed early, because Papa Is wanted us to try to understand that there would be changes in our lives now. These changes would be difficult ones, too. If we didn't *always* obey him or Annie, it might be very bad for all of us.

When bedtime finally came, Papa Is took me to bed while Gerda waited in the other room with Annie. He spoke to me softly. "Dotje, we must talk about you, about your being Jewish. You know, being Jewish today is very difficult, and one must have a good deal of courage to be proud of being a Jew. It is very important for you to remember that the Germans do not like the Jews, and that includes you—just for the simple reason that you are Jewish. I don't know why exactly, but perhaps it's because they just need a group of people to pick on, to conquer, or to destroy to show how great and strong they are. We know they are wrong, but we are not quite strong enough to stop them just yet, so you must listen carefully to what I tell you. Whatever the reason, sometimes the Germans look for any excuse to hurt Jews. It's important to me that this doesn't happen to you, for I love you very much. From now on, you must not only be very good, but you must always do everything I say, quickly and without questioning me. Let's both say a little prayer that they will soon leave all the Jews alone."

My throat was in a knot. I had a million questions for Papa Is, but he wanted no questions. Instead, my head screamed, "What about Joseph?" "Have they hurt Mama and Papa in Goch?" How will they hurt us?" "What will they do?" "Who will tell them we are Jewish?" "What is bad about being Jewish?" "Why aren't you and Gerda and Annie Jewish? Did you choose not to be Jewish?"

Papa Is left the room slowly. He said that tomorrow I would begin a new school, but Gerda wouldn't be going with me. My new school was for Jewish children only, for this was the way the Germans wanted it. He said that if I was very good and worked very hard, I might again start learning to read. There were two things I must now always remember. The first was that I had to wear a yellow Star of David on my clothes. He said this was a German rule and all the Jews in Amsterdam were required to do this. Jews all over Europe were wearing stars too—on their coats, shirts, suits, and dresses. The Germans would arrest any Jew who didn't wear the six-pointed yellow star. This did not really sound like a bad rule because I liked being Jewish. I didn't think I would mind wearing the Star of David on my clothes. "There's one other thing, Dotje," Papa Is continued. "If anybody, no matter how young or old, calls you a dirty Jew, or shouts at you, or hits you, or even throws stones at you, you are never, *never* to fight back! Do you understand, Dotje? Do you understand?"

I remembered that Joseph had asked me whether anyone had ever called me a dirty Jew. I didn't expect it to happen to me at all, but I told Papa Is that I would not fight back if it did. This was not enough. He made me tell him again and again until I became afraid. He kissed me goodnight and hugged me too hard. I shall not forget that night.

I saw two of my cousins the next day at the Jewish school. They and all the other children were wearing stars. There were forty-two of us, and we were seated in one large room. Just as lessons were about to begin, a German officer walked into the room and smiled. My heart began pounding, and I was afraid he could hear it. He spoke softly and asked us to take off our coats. Then he put his hands behind his back and walked slowly up and down the aisles between our desks. Annie had sewn a yellow star on my coat and

my dress, but seven children didn't have stars on their dresses and shirts. He stopped at their desks one at a time and wished them, "Good morning." He bent over and told them that they were special children, and would be excused from school that day. He asked them to put on their coats again and come with him. He said he was going to drive them home in his large car, but I never ever saw them again.

The next day fourteen children came to school, but no German officer visited us. Our teacher called him "Gestapo." I learned to hate the Gestapo, the Nazi secret police, more than Haman of Bible times hated the Jews. I wished that I could stamp out the name "Gestapo" just as we used to stamp out Haman's name when the Bible story of Queen Esther was read aloud in the synagogue on the holiday of Purim. We used to drown out Haman's name with noisemakers and the stamping of many feet, but now I was one little girl alone. The day passed quickly, and when class was out I started to run home to tell Papa Is what I had learned. On the way, I saw a friend whom we had skated with during the winter. He was on his bicycle and I started to call to him, but suddenly he raced his bicycle toward me. Before I could leap aside, he steered the front wheel into me and knocked me down. He stopped long enough to spit on my cheek and shout, "You dumb, stupid, dirty Jew!" His spit ran into my ear, and I began to cry. It had happened so fast. I hadn't hit back—I hadn't even thought of it. I couldn't understand why he hated me so. When he was out of sight, I ran home and fell into Papa Is' arms. "Please take my star off! Please! Please! I don't want to be a Jew anymore!" Papa Is did not answer. He just held me as I cried.

* * *

By the end of the second week of school there were only nine children attending class, and Annie decided that it was too dangerous for me to go anymore. I would miss learning, but it was true I was afraid to walk home alone. Now I would stay near the apartment and practice my ice-skating. The next day I learned I could no longer go to the canal. Papa Is told me that Jewish children were not allowed to ice-skate anymore. I could only stand near the edge of the canal and watch the others glide by. I asked Annie if I could go to the playground near the school, but she said that Jewish children were not allowed to play there anymore. Papa Is and I went for a long walk. He had not yet told me that those with yellow Stars of David could no longer walk on the sidewalks. We walked silently along the gutter holding hands.

Jewish Quotas

I had never heard the word "quota" before, but now everyone was speaking of quotas. Annie said that each day the Germans made new quotas for the Jews in Amsterdam. She explained that quotas were amounts or numbers, but it still was not clear at first. Tonight the quota had been five Jews per street and one person per house. I began to understand but still wondered why they kept changing the quotas. Papa Is explained. The Nazis wanted to keep everyone uncertain and off-balance. When people expect something to happen in a certain way, they are not very frightened, but when rules and laws and quotas are constantly changed, no one knows what to expect and every moment brings fear and insecurity.

Sometimes the Nazis came to collect quotas in the early evening around supper time. Other times they would wake us at three o'clock in the morning. They were always changing the time. The changes worked just as Papa Is said. We were all becoming very frightened. Since the Gestapo had lists of all the Jewish people who lived in Amsterdam, we never knew whether they were coming to collect only Jews or a certain number of people on a certain street. When they came, it was like a round-up.

Papa Is called the round-up a "razzia," the German word for a police raid. At the razzia, they rounded up everyone, but they didn't want everyone; and they would never tell us until it was too late. The round-up would begin when the Germans closed off a certain block at both ends by parking large trucks in the middle of the street. The trucks were loaded with soldiers and had big machine guns on top of the cab. Some of the soldiers would leave the trucks and climb onto our roofs carrying other machine guns to point into the street. That way they would be certain that no one could escape. Other truckloads of soldiers came. They carried small machine guns under their arms and raced into all our homes. We would be made to go out into the street in the cold without having time to put on our coats. Sometimes we would have to stand in the street for many hours and just shiver. Usually, those non-Jews who had their papers in order were allowed to leave the street quickly. We Jews had to just stand and wait until the soldiers loaded as many of us as they wished into large cattle trucks to be taken away somewhere. Those of us still left in the street were allowed to return home. We lived in constant fear that we would be loaded into one of the trucks and taken away.

I remember how brave Annie was, now that I think back on that first razzia. The Gestapo had pushed open our door and demanded that all four of us go out into the street. She showed them her papers and Papa Is' too. Then they asked for Gerda's and mine. Annie handed Gerda's papers to them and began explaining that we were all Dutch citizens and had a right to remain in our home. She talked and talked, and we did not move. She was frightened when they shouted and pointed to me, but somehow she talked them out of taking any of us. All of a sudden they seemed satisfied, turned around, and were gone.

For me, the second razzia was worse. It was late one night when they came. They closed off the street and turned huge spotlights toward the apartment houses. Papa Is and Annie lifted me onto a narrow folding bed and strapped me securely to the mattress. Then they closed me up into the closet and told me not to make a sound. I could hear the Gestapo's loud stomping boots on the stairs and the banging on the door. They came in and searched everywhere. They even opened the closet where I was and for a moment I froze. Then they closed the door and left without saying a word. I was safe once again.

I prayed that God would stop the Germans from frightening me so much, but God must have been very busy with many other more important prayers, for He did not answer mine.

Several days went by and we began to relax a little. Then they came a third time. At first, no one could think of a place for me to hide and I started to panic. Papa Is cried in a harsh whisper, "The attic!" I was boosted through a tiny trapdoor into the small attic. Annie directed me toward a splintery wooden box. She told me to climb into it and pull the top down over my head. I had to crouch to get the top down, but I was too afraid to be uncomfortable.

Once again the Gestapo searched our rooms. They stayed even longer this time, as though they knew someone was hiding somewhere. After a while, they seemed satisfied and they left. It took me quite a while to stop trembling, but I didn't cry a tear. Annie said I was a very brave girl, and that she was quite proud of me. I thought that perhaps now, since they had searched our house so much, they would leave us alone and start searching other houses. I guess I didn't realize that they already were searching other homes.

The fourth razzia was a total surprise. The Nazis were unusually quiet. It was on a Sunday afternoon and no one expected them. Annie was sewing, and Papa Is was reading when they knocked lightly at the door. Then they were inside the house before one could catch a breath. This time Annie was her very bravest. As one of the four soldiers grabbed my arm, Annie screamed at them, "You ought to be ashamed of yourselves! What kind of men are you, trying to take such an innocent little girl!" Papa Is stood motionless with his arms around Gerda. Suddenly, the soldier let go of my arm and said that he didn't like doing these things any more than we did, for he had two little girls at home, but he was only following orders. The four just turned and left. I trembled in the middle of the floor. I didn't think of Joseph now or of Mama and Papa in Goch either. I just thought of hiding. I wanted to hide deep inside of something and be able to cover myself so well that no one in the entire world would ever find me. Annie handed me a large piece of chocolate. I tried to eat it, but I could not swallow.

It was quiet for nine days. There had been fewer and fewer razzias, and I thought they were finally going to stop them. Papa Is said that there were fewer round-ups because there were fewer Jews to round up. Now there were rumors that the Gestapo were beginning to check the town lists for names of individual Jews they had missed during the razzias.

The fifth time the soldiers came to our house was just before curfew. The Germans had set a curfew when they first arrived in Amsterdam. By seven o'clock in the evening, everyone had to be off the streets or they would be arrested. Annie was at a neighbor's house, and we expected her back any minute. I remember the night was a bitter cold one. They didn't knock this time. Five of them just pushed the door open and shouted, "Where is Dotje Cohen!" Papa Is began to scream and shout at them. He even hit two of them, but they just laughed and knocked him down. Annie was on the stairs. I squeezed my fingers into my fists to keep from screaming. She heard the noise and came running, but it was too late. They were taking me away and Annie could do nothing about it. She made them wait a few moments while she packed a small sweater and a few other bits of clothing into a tiny suitcase. One of the soldiers grabbed it and pushed it at me. Then he started pushing me down the stairs. The stairs were dark and I couldn't see; I kept stumbling on my suitcase. I didn't feel the bitter cold because I was so afraid. I was more afraid the night they took me away from my foster family than I had ever been in my whole life.

The Concentration Camp

A blast of icy air hit me as I stepped into the street, and I shivered. I was boosted up into the back of a big cattle truck, and my bundle was tossed in after me. The back gate of the truck was fastened and locked. The soldiers climbed into the truck's cab, and we began to move. There were others in the back with me, but it was too dark to recognize any of them, and besides, it was freezing cold. Although I was in the truck for almost a half-hour, our final stop was only two houses down from our apartment.

We were all pushed and shoved into a giant room. I remember it was huge, but there was no furniture, only people. We were in that room only a short while, and then they began the separations. There are days now when I can still hear the screaming in my ears, but for me it was not as bad as for some of the others. My mother and father would not have to suffer like the mothers and fathers I watched. The Gestapo had decided that all the parents must give up their children, and one by one, they called their names. Soldiers dragged the children away from their parents into another large room. I heard mothers pleading and fathers crying to be taken instead, but it did no good. When they called my name I went and was grateful Mama and Papa weren't there. Oh God, they kept crying and crying. . . .

It had been hours now since I had been taken from Annie and Papa Is, and I had to go to the bathroom. I walked slowly to a Gestapo officer and asked him if I could go to the bathroom. I had asked in Dutch and he did not understand. I didn't remember my German any longer, but I tried again in Dutch. This time he became angry at my bothering him, so he hit me. I didn't know he had hit me at first, for it happened so quickly. The blow from the butt of his rifle to my forehead knocked me over, yet I felt no pain! It was only when my eye felt wet a few moments later, and I tried to wipe the wetness away, that I realized it was blood. I began to cry. Tears mixed with the blood and dripped onto my dress. I pulled off my dirty scarf and tried to stop the bleeding by holding it on the deep wound. The soldier came back, for he was not yet through with me. Now he understood that I had to go to the bathroom and he dragged me toward the stalls. I went into the nearest one and closed the door. He pushed it open behind me, and then he laughed. . . .

The Separation

The next day all the children were loaded into the cattle trucks. The mothers and fathers began screaming again for their children, and we could hear them as we pulled away. It was still very cold outside, but it felt very good on my swollen head. The blood had dried and formed a scab on my forehead and into my hair. "When I get home, Annie will help me clean it," I thought, but I should have known better. I would not be going home. I squatted down in the truck and the wind was not as sharp. Others squatted down too, and their bodies felt warm. I was glad that I wasn't alone.

Someone called the place we were taken to a detention camp, but it looked just like a group of houses. They were rundown, but at one time, I was certain, they had been very beautiful. Now there was a gigantic fence around them with eight strands of barbed wire. Where there had been gardens, there was just dirt and gravel. German signs were posted everywhere, and I did not know what to expect.

I was surprised to find that Jewish girls were put in charge of us. As we were unloaded from the trucks, a girl named Esther told us to follow her into one of the buildings. She was beginning to explain the camp rules to us when a German officer marched into the room. "Achtung!" he shouted, and we watched Esther leap to her feet and raise her hand. He shouted again. "Achtung!" This time we followed her example, We scrambled to our feet and awkwardly raised our hands. He seemed pleased. He turned and left.

I was in the detention camp a total of eight weeks. My head slowly healed, but only because God cared for it when no one else would. I remembered Papa telling me Bible stories about how God had cared for Ruth when she was in a strange land and for King David when he was in the wilderness. I prayed that God would somehow take care of me, too.

There were lice in my hair and it itched all the time. There was no way to wash it. They had probably come from sleeping on the floor each night. We were allowed to use some straw under our coats for a mattress, but it didn't work very well. Each morning I would eat breakfast next to one of the new friends I made at the camp. We were given a piece of black bread and some jelly. Our lunch was the same thing. For supper they brought us a tin cup of soup. At bedtime, I would try to find one of my friends to sleep with, but each day the Gestapo kept taking them away. I was beginning to wish they would take me. Early each morning they would read the list of names, and then another friend would get ready to leave to go to another resettlement camp. As they left, I became lonely and afraid again.

One day, to my amazement, Joseph sneaked into camp. I will never know how he found out where I was or how he got past the carefully guarded gates or the incredibly high wire. I cried and I cried. He held me in his arms just as Papa would have done. He stayed with me for almost six hours, and we talked about everything. Esther saw him, but said nothing. I kissed his arms and dirty hands and put them around me. I breathed his dirty hair and soiled clothes, and stopped being afraid for a while. It was getting dark when he finally told me he must go. He said he would try to see me again soon, but if he couldn't, I mustn't worry. He rubbed the almost healed crooked scab on my forehead and kissed me some more. Then he was gone. I might not have let him go had I known how many years would pass before I would see my brother Joseph again.

Two days later they called my name. I packed my few belongings and climbed onto the cattle truck along with seventeen others. We traveled for three hours before we stopped near a railway station. German soldiers marched us toward a long train. The grown-ups began to cry softly. They knew about the trains. Some children tugged on their parents' coats and asked where the trains were going. Parents just hugged their children more closely to them and did not answer. I remembered stories from neighbors in Amsterdam. People said that the trains were taking all the Jews to their death. They spoke of death camps, crematoriums, and the showers. One thing we all knew—no Jews ever returned from the showers. One thing we all knew—no Jews ever returned from the camps.

We were marched onto a long platform next to open boxcars. They grabbed us one by one and shoved us into the boxcars. When my turn came, it appeared that God took charge of me once more, for a real miracle happened. They had just taken the boy in front of me and an officer was holding tightly onto my hand so I wouldn't squirm away. In a split second, a stranger who was walking by grabbed my hand away from the officer, and in a flash we were moving away from the train station! I didn't know who he was and I was breathless trying to keep up with him.

We went on and on, and he never said a word. We went through weeds and farm fields. We went through mud and over rocks. After what seemed like endless running we reached a thick forest, and he said, "Rest a moment."

To this day I do not know the name of the stranger who rescued me from certain death, except that he belonged to the underground. It was dark and I was asleep when he carried me back to Annie and Papa Is. They both kissed me and we cried. I wanted to be put right to bed, but Annie scrubbed me and scrubbed me. She washed my hair with awful-smelling shampoo and made noisy grunts about the lice. My eyes burned. My skin felt stretched by the time she was through with me. She wrapped me in a large warm towel and gave me to Papa Is. He carried me into my old small bed and tucked me in. It was like finding my secret hiding place to be back home. Gerda was lying next to me in her bed already asleep. I, too, fell asleep before I could enjoy the full impact of being home once again.

Amsterdam

Pain and suffering was not over for me or for the other Jews in Amsterdam. We were not the only ones to suffer now, however. The Germans had broken many of the dikes when they took over the country, and now much of Holland's farmland was flooded. People slowly began to starve.

I had to stay in our house all of the time. I was supposed to be dead as far as the Germans were concerned, and we were afraid that if the neighbors saw me they would tell the soldiers for an extra ration of food. There was not much to do to keep busy, but I behaved very well. I watched Papa Is stitch clothes for the neighbors and for Gerda and me. I helped Annie clean the apartment, too. Often Annie and Gerda went into the country with some of Annie's fine linens. She would find a farm which had not been flooded by the broken dikes and would trade the linens for a few potatoes and some sugar beets. I can still remember eating those sugar beets. Annie mashed them and baked them. She fried them and cooked them into a soup. Once she even made them into muffins so they would taste different. They always tasted the same to me and gave me severe stomach cramps, but how we all laughed when she tried to color them red to change the taste.

In a few months all the linens were gone. There was nothing else to trade with the farmers, so we had no more to eat and Papa Is didn't know what to do. Then something good happened, although to you, dear children, it will sound quite bad. When the Germans broke the dikes, it caused the sewage to mix with the clean drinking water so that the people couldn't drink it anymore. Dirty water flowed into the streets, and the stink came into the windows. Tulip bulbs which had been planted the past spring loosened and rotted on the sidewalks. Rats gorged themselves on the bulbs and garbage, grew fat, and died. All of Amsterdam was starving, but now the people were able to survive. They lived because they gathered the fat dead rats and the rotted tulip bulbs and made soup. No one asked what was in the soup; we just ate it hungrily. Now and then each family managed to get a few tulip bulbs which were not rotten, and we would nibble on one when we became too hungry. They swelled up in our stomachs and caused us great pain after we ate them, so we ate as few as possible.

It was in the middle of this terrible hunger that Beertje came to live with us. Beertje was Papa Is' nephew, and he was just eighteen months old. His family lived across the courtyard from us, and sometimes we would visit them. One night while we were all sleeping, the Gestapo came for Beertje's parents. Beertje was asleep and never made a sound. The Gestapo didn't even notice him as they dragged his parents away. The next morning we heard him crying and Papa Is went to get him, and he came to live with us. His mother and father never returned. I learned to love Beertje a lot, and it became my job to care for him when Annie was away. It was important to keep him as quiet as possible so that the neighbors would forget that he lived with us. I was always afraid for him.

While I played with Beertje each day, Papa Is built me a cupboard. It was a hiding cupboard above his closet and was just big enough to crouch in if the Gestapo came to look for me again. He told me it was a special cupboard just for me and that I should use it only if I had to. Some days I would practice hiding, and Papa Is would make me climb over the top of the closet quickly to get to it. It was very dark in there and I felt crunched, but I knew it was more than a game and I stayed very quiet until Papa Is told me to come out. My back would hurt from stooping so long, but Papa Is would rub it while Beertje gurgled.

The nights were cold for both Jews and Christians. The Germans had taken all our fuel to keep their soldiers warm, and now all of Amsterdam shivered. Families would get together at night and huddle around a single table where a small sterno light would burn. This was our only warmth, and we kept our coats on all night long. Children slept in their parents' arms but still shivered. We could no longer use the bathroom because of the problem caused by the broken dikes, so we all used a can in the bedroom to relieve ourselves. Papa Is hauled drinking water from the only clean well left in Amsterdam, which was in the center of the city. Our days were cold and hungry. I played with Beertje and dreamed of Joseph. Then one day it was spring.

Jewish Partisans

I had heard Annie and Papa Is whispering to each other about Joseph. They said he was in a concentration camp just outside Amsterdam. They had been trying to find out how he was. Unfortunately, they had not received any news. Papa Is said Joseph might survive because he was a strong boy. Those who were strong survived longer. I prayed that Joseph was strong, but I knew that even the strongest needed food to survive, and Annie said that there was very little food for the prisoners. Even the strongest needed a place to sleep and medical care. I asked God to help Joseph survive until the war was over and we could be together again.

It was Papa Is who first spoke to friends of Beertje's parents. Beertje's father was in the same camp as Joseph, Papa Is learned. Beertje's mother was dead. She had been expecting another baby and she died when it was born. I was sad to think of little Beertje not having a mother and a new baby to play with. Beertje's father and Joseph had worked together for several weeks. Then Joseph suddenly disappeared.

We tried to learn more about Joseph's disappearance. We didn't know whether he was ill or had died like so many others. Was it possible he had escaped? Annie was certain that there had been no escape, for, she said, no one ever escaped from the camps. Why, then, couldn't we get news of him?

More and more we began to hear the word "partisan." Always it was said in a whisper, with a backwards glance to be certain no one else was listening. In the faraway ghettos of Warsaw and Bialystok in Poland, we learned, brave Jews were fighting the Nazis. They fought with a courage born of desperation; they were fighting not only for their own survival, but for the survival and the honor of the Jewish people. The partisans were also fighting to save the Jewish people and to bring down the hated Nazi regime. Usually, they would band together and hide in the forest, coming out at night to attack.

Nine long years would pass before we learned that Joseph had been saved from certain death by a group of Jewish partisans. They had bribed the German guards to save Joseph, nineteen other young boys, and six girls. The partisans believed that these children were the future of the Jewish people. They felt that it was worth risking their lives to save the children.

When such escapes did occur, they were usually made right before the Germans' eyes. Bribed guards would often march a group of escapees right through a main gate and load them onto a truck. Bribed drivers would drive them to a prearranged vantage point, and from there the youths would work their way through the dark night until the Jewish partisans found them. That was how it was with Joseph and his group. But danger was never far behind those who escaped. Even after the partisans helped to guide and protect them, they would have to go days without rest and with only small amounts of food. They would hide in cramped places by day and travel over difficult terrain by night. On the final leg of their journey, they traveled on boats which rocked until most of them were ill. It wasn't until they reached Palestine and spent weeks with new "families" that they felt happy to be alive once again.

Joseph made such a journey, but I had lost all contact with him. It took many years of letters and persistent inquiries before I learned that Joseph was alive and well. He was a member of Israel's underground army, the Haganah. It was many more years before the two of us met in Jerusalem, the capital of Israel.

After the War

I was thirteen years old when the war ended. It was in May 1945. Hundreds of people poured into the streets, dancing happily despite the filth and the dead rats. They built bonfires and clapped and sang. Since 1940, when the Germans had arrived, no Dutch flags had flown in Holland. Now they were everywhere, and the people shouted as they hung them up.

One last tragedy occurred before the people could really begin to rebuild their lives. When the news came that the Germans had been defeated, we all ran to the center of town to celebrate. There in the square, the mayor was speaking to the people about the future of Amsterdam and of peace. In the middle of his speech, Annie came rushing after Gerda and me. She grabbed our arms and insisted we return home. We both screamed angrily at her, but she was most insistent and dragged us away. We were almost home when we heard the awful screams and the machine guns. Yes, the war was over, but the Germans had not finished their killing. Three German tanks had pushed their way into the town square. They stopped and aimed. Then they killed and they killed. Two hundred and sixty-eight Dutch men, women, and children were killed in a little over fifteen minutes on that day of great celebration. The war was over, and Amsterdam mourned its dead.

American soldiers arrived two days later, and we lined up along the streets to welcome them. They stopped their tanks and gave us gifts of chewing gum, cans of meat, and dried eggs. Now there was food everywhere, but for starving people, too much food too soon can be dangerous. Once again Annie interfered and saved our lives.

After we were liberated, the Red Cross dropped CARE packages filled with delicious, nourishing food all over Holland. Annie wouldn't allow us to eat more than a few spoonfuls twice a day. We hated her for it until we learned that our neighbors were dying from eating too much. It was very lucky that Annie was so wise.

Yes, she was very wise, and she had saved my life many times. I was very grateful to her and wanted to spend the rest of my life helping her with the chores and cleaning her house. I could have helped Papa Is, too, for his eyes were not as sharp as they had been, and sometimes he didn't stitch straight and I had to undo his stitches so he could do them again. I knew he needed me, but Annie didn't. I loved Beertje and wanted to take care of him until he grew up tall and strong. Gerda wouldn't mind my staying if I helped her always put her things away, but Annie didn't want me now that the war was over. She had given more than most, and now she was done giving. It was time for me to go.

Household School

Papa Is and Annie began the difficult task of writing letters and sending them all over the world to see whether any of my relatives were still alive somewhere. Once I finally realized that Papa Is and Annie weren't going to keep me, I began to hope that they wouldn't find anybody to take their place. I wanted to go to Israel with the other war orphans. I had been hated so much because I was a Jew that now I just wanted to be in a place where there were only Jews.

While I waited for plans to be made for me, it was decided that I should go to Household School. I was too old for elementary school, even though I had never had a real chance to learn and had only been allowed to attend for a few weeks.

Household School was a place where children learned how to be maids. I didn't mind going, but I wished that I could learn to read. They said they were going to teach me, but they didn't. I was thirteen and still couldn't read. I began to think I wasn't smart enough. At Household School I learned how to sew, I learned how to clean thoroughly, and I learned how to cook. I sewed and cleaned and cooked for two years, but I still couldn't read.

Just before I left the school, one of my roommates called me a dirty Jew. Nothing like this had happened since the end of the war. Papa Is' lesson about never fighting back flashed through my head. Now it was different; there was no war, and I lost control. I took off my wooden shoe and hit her head. Then I hit her and I hit her. I could see that she was bloody, and I think I heard her screaming, but I just kept beating her. It took two people to pull me away and drag me into the principal's office. I knew I had been wrong, and I was ready for the worst. Instead, the principal seemed to understand, and he was very kind. He explained that if I planned to hit everyone who called me a bad name, I would be leaving a trail of bloody faces wherever I went. I promised that I would try to follow his advice. The other girl was dismissed from school, and I never saw her again.

I left school at the end of my second year and was preparing to go to Israel with a group of two hundred other orphan children when the letter came.

They had found a relative. It was an aunt who lived in a country called Mexico. She had written to Papa Is and said that she would not only take me but also all the other Cohen children. She didn't know yet that Mama and Papa were dead and Joseph's whereabouts unknown. All my cousins were dead, too. I was the only Cohen child.

I don't remember packing or saying goodbye to Annie, Gerda, and Papa Is. I couldn't understand why they didn't want me anymore. I don't remember traveling to Mexico, but I do remember how beautiful it was! It was a country of flowers and friendly people. And Aunt Sarah was a real relative. It didn't take me long to learn to love her, for she was very good to me. Her husband, whom I called just "Uncle," was also very kind. He kept insisting that I go to school. I didn't want to. "Uncle, I am almost sixteen and have never learned to read. Don't you see—I am dumb and can't learn. Please don't make me go to school!" He answered gruffly, "Let me be the judge of how dumb you are!" And the next day my lessons began.

I studied German, French, Spanish, and English every day for five hours. I studied math and, best of all, I studied reading. I had arrived in Mexico in May. By September, my tutor felt I was ready for second grade. I am certain you have never known anyone who studied as hard as I did. Once I was allowed to really learn, I worked and I worked. Sometimes Uncle would find me at my books long after the entire tiny town was asleep; but my hard work paid off. By the time I was seventeen, I was able to graduate to sixth grade with high honors. I remember the gift from Aunt Sarah and Uncle as if it were yesterday. It was a brand-new baby doll, my first one ever. They were trying to give me a little piece of the childhood I had never known.

*   *   *

There is more, but you don't have to know the rest. What is important is that I have shared my story. It was not an easy story to tell. As I told it, many sad thoughts came back to me, and I felt much of my pain again. But pain is a small price to pay when I think that perhaps you will not forget my story. I pray that when you grow up you will see to it that such a horrible thing as the Holocaust never happens again. No one believed it could happen, but it did. Please, *please* try with all your might to see that it doesn't happen again. *Please!*

EPILOGUE

Jewish refugees landing in the port of Haifa.

A Jewish Homeland

Dotje's story had a happy ending, but what of the thousands of other Jewish children caught in the war? Where did they go? How did they live? Who took care of them? Most of all, who wanted these orphans and who would love them?

The orphaned children who had no place to go after the war, no place to call home, were sent to the land of Palestine, which today we know as the State of Israel. Many brave men and women—people who felt that children were very important—helped to smuggle these young Jews into the land that became the Jewish state. When they arrived, homes were found for them, and they were cared for, loved, and protected from harm. Soon they were no longer afraid, and they began to grow strong and healthy once again.

Jewish refugees on their way to Palestine.

You have learned about the "lucky" children, the orphans like Joseph who were smuggled directly into the promised land—Palestine, the future State of Israel. But others were forced to take a longer route and their journey was a very difficult and dangerous one.

In 1947, Palestine was ruled by the British and they would not allow Jewish refugees to settle there. The British did not want to upset the Arabs.

British soldiers with guard dogs searching for illegal Jewish immigrants.

The *Haganah*, a Jewish self-defense force, organized an "illegal" immigration into Palestine. Jewish refugees—men, women, and children— were taken to a city in France called Marseilles. There they secretly boarded rusty, old ships for the trip to Palestine. Most of these boats were caught by the British navy and forced to sail to the island of Cyprus. There the refugees were placed in *displaced persons (D.P.) camps*.

The camps for displaced persons were very much like the concentration camps they had just left. There was a huge barbed-wire fence surrounding the camp, and armed British soldiers with guard dogs watched the people very closely.

A displaced persons camp on the island of Cyprus.

In the camps, there were about twenty children to each tent. They were from different countries, they spoke different languages, but they all had one thing in common. All of them were orphans, no fathers, no mothers, no sisters, no brothers, no relatives. Their families had been murdered by the Nazis. They were the only survivors. Even now, they were being denied the chance to build a new home in Israel, the only country in the world where they were welcome.

The refugee boat Exodus 1947. *It was this boat that the British refused permission to enter Palestine.*

Thousands of other displaced persons were even less lucky than those sent by the British to Cyprus. In the summer of 1947, a rusty, old ship with more than five thousand refugees tried to land in Palestine. This ship was called the *Exodus 1947*. Within sight of the promised land, armed British sailors boarded the ship and told the passengers that they would not be permitted to enter Palestine. They would have to turn back and return home.

Jewish refugees imprisoned in a British camp in Germany.

The angry unarmed survivors of the death camps fought the armed British sailors with their bare hands. Jews were killed and wounded. The *Exodus* was forced to sail back to France. However, the passengers refused to leave their ship. They had boarded the *Exodus* for Palestine and they would not leave until they entered their homeland. Now, the *Exodus* was forced to sail to Hamburg, Germany. There the Jews were removed from the boat by force. Armed British soldiers carried the refugees off the ship and then imprisoned them in a British displaced persons camp in Germany.

Jewish children in Israel learning the Hebrew language.

It was then that all the Jewish people in the world experienced a great blessing. In May of 1948 the State of Israel was born. Now Jews the world over had a true homeland, a place where one could be proud of being Jewish, a place to call their own. If other countries didn't want the Jews, Israel did. Any Jew could become a citizen of the new state, and Jews were wanted, really wanted.

They came from everywhere—from Europe, from Africa, from Asia, from any country you can name. And the State of Israel grew and became strong. Life wasn't always easy, for many things had to be done to help the country grow and prosper. A good democratic government had to be formed, land had to be cleared for farming, homes and schools had to be built, roads cleared, hospitals erected, synagogues started, and the new immigrants cared for. But people work very hard when they are free, and the Jewish people valued their freedom as sacred. Soon the land began to bloom. Orchards filled the countryside and crops grew well. Children studied their lessons and worked in the fields. Men built homes by day and became soldiers to guard their new country by night. Women cared for their homes and children, and also helped the sick. Sometimes they worked in the fields or helped the men guard their homes and the land. Everyone worked hard, but everyone was very happy and very thankful that after thousands of years, there was finally a Jewish state in Israel.

Today, Israel continues to grow and prosper. The country has problems, but its people are working hard to keep their land strong and secure. We hope that we may answer Dotje's prayers by helping to keep Israel a safe haven for Jews who wish to live there. Above all, we pray that Israel will help the world to make sure that there is never again a tragedy like the Holocaust.

GLOSSARY

Anti-Semitism. Prejudice and hatred for Jews.

Bomb shelters. Specially constructed areas used to protect people from falling bombs during air raids.

CARE. American organization that sent packages of food and clothing to help the people in Europe after World War II.

Challah. Special bread used on Shabbat (the Jewish Sabbath) and Yom Tov (Jewish holidays).

Cholent. A Jewish Sabbath dish made of potatoes, beans, and meat cooked all night.

Concentration camp. A special prison camp where the Nazis sent Jews and other people.

Crematorium. An oven used in death camps to burn the bodies of Jews killed in the gas chambers.

Deportation. The act of forcing a group of people to leave a country.

Dike. An embankment or dam erected to prevent flooding by the sea or a river.

Esther. In the Bible, the Jewish heroine who brought about the downfall of Haman. *See* Purim.

Foster parent. Substitute parent.

Gestapo. Nazi secret police.

Ghetto. Area in a city where only certain groups of people can live.

Haganah. The underground Jewish army in Palestine.

Haman. *See* Purim.

Hasidic. Term applied to Jews who belong to the group known as Hasidim, a very pious sect that was founded in Eastern Europe in the eighteenth century. Hasidic Jews wear distinctive clothing and have many distinctive practices.

High Holy Days. The Jewish holidays of Rosh Hashanah (New Year) and Yom Kippur (Day of Atonement).

Hitler, Adolf. The leader of Nazi Germany from 1933 to 1945.

Holocaust. The destruction of six million Jewish men, women, and children by the Nazis during World War II.

Household school. A school for training housemaids.

Jewish State. Another term for the State of Israel, the independent Jewish national homeland, in the Near East.

Kiddush cup. A cup used in the Jewish ceremony of kiddush (blessing over the wine) on the Sabbath and holidays.

Kristallnacht. German for "Night of Broken Glass." An organized attack against the Jews of Germany on November 9–10, 1939.

Natural causes. A term generally used in describing deaths occurring normally from illness, old age, etc., as compared to deaths resulting from accidents, violent crime, and war. The Nazis tried to speed up the process of death from "natural" causes by depriving the Jews in the ghettos of food, warm clothing, medicine and other necessities. When this didn't kill enough Jews fast enough, the Nazis began using firing squads and gas chambers instead.

Nazis. Members of the Nazi Party, the anti-Semitic political group headed by Adolf Hitler.

Orphan. A child whose parents are dead.

Parachute. Large umbrella-shaped cloth device used for jumping from an airplane.

Partisan. An underground or guerilla fighter.

Passover. One of the three Jewish "pilgrimage festivals," occurring in the spring. It commemorates the liberation of the children of Israel from slavery in ancient Egypt.

Persecution. The constant tormenting of a people, for religious, racial, or other reasons, in order to harm them or to prevent them from leading normal lives as full members of society. During much of their history in Europe, the Jews, as a minority subjected to many unfair laws and restrictions, were a persecuted people.

Pogrom. An organized attack against Jews.

Purim. Jewish holiday celebrating the rescue of the Jews of Persia from the evil Haman.

Quota. The number of people to be selected for some purpose, such as to be sent to a concentration camp.

Ration. A fixed portion or amount of food assigned to a person during wartime or other periods of shortage.

Razzia. German word for police raid or round-up.

Resettlement camp. False name given by the Nazis to the death camps.

Resistance. A term generally applied to underground fighting organizations (guerrillas) and other means used by a people to assert their identity, protect their life-style and values, and thwart the intentions of a conquering or persecuting power.

Romans. European empire that ruled much of the ancient world.

Rosh Hashanah. Jewish New Year.

Second Temple. After the Jews returned to Israel from the Babylonian exile, they built a new temple to replace the one destroyed by the Babylonians. This second temple was destroyed in 70 C.E. by the Romans when the Jewish attempt to gain national independence was defeated.

Shabbat. The Jewish Sabbath (occurs on Saturday).

Shema. Important Jewish prayer.

Shavuot. One of the three Jewish "pilgrimage festivals," occurring at the beginning of summer. In English it is sometimes called Pentecost or Weeks.

Sukkot. One of the three Jewish "pilgrimage festivals," occurring in the autumn. In English it is sometimes called Tabernacles or Booths.

Tisha B'Av. A solemn fast-day, occurring on the ninth day of the Hebrew month of Av (July-August), commemorating the destruction of the First Temple in 586 B.C.E. and the Second Temple in 70 C.E.

Waiting station. A place where Jewish refugee children from Germany had to wait until they were sent to foster families.

Yom Kippur. Day of Atonement, one of the holiest days in the Jewish calendar.